MEMORIES of New Brancepeth

John Kitching

Published by
COUNTY DURHAM BOOKS

Cover: **Eshwood Street in 1911**, the group of children on the left are standing outside the post office, also to the left is the Wesleyan church built at a cost of £580 in 1877, having a capacity for 250 worshippers. Opposite is Mr. Harold Gardiners beer shop where a delivery is being made by Vaux's horse drawn dray.

Acknowledgments

My sincere thanks are due to the following institutes and individuals.

Arts, Libraries & Museums Department
Durham County Council.

Beamish, North of England Open Air Museum.

Mrs. G. R. Ives
Mr. G. Nairn
Mr. K. Clark
Mr. R. Kitching
Mr. M. Richardson
Mr. J. Bell
Mr. W. Taylor
Mr. D. Schofield
Mrs. D. Fox - Vaux Group P.L.C.

And most of all, my family for their support & enthusiasm

© JR Kitching County Durham Books, 1997.

Published by Durham County Council:
Arts, Libraries & Museums Department, 1997.

Printed by Reprographic Section

ISBN 1-897585-38-1

The Colliery village of New Brancepeth or Sleetburn as it was formally known is situated on the South side of the Deerness Valley.

Alexander Brodie Cochrane who came from Staffordshire took a lease on the Hall at Aldin Grange, near Bearpark in the middle of the 19th Century. He also obtained the rights to mine for coal at New Brancepeth from Lord Boyne of Brancepeth Castle who held the Royalties.

He built a house near to his colliery called Eshwood Hall. The Cochrane family had an iron works at Ormesby, on the banks of the Tees, and the top quality coking coal produced at New Brancepeth colliery supplied the needs of the iron works. The first shaft was started in 1856 with the first coal being drawn from the busty steam in 1858. This shaft was closed after a couple of years due to a geological fault. During this time coal was won from the drifts along the side of the valley, until 1865 when the Brockwell seam was reached at 70 fathoms. The third shaft was sunk in 1872 to the Victoria seam, at 76 fathoms.

Other seams worked at New Brancepeth colliery were The Hutton, Harvey and three-quarter seams. By 1913, The colliery had developed into a large complex, with brickworks, brytes crushing plant, (a heavy mineral first discovered at New Brancepeth in 1900) in vertical seams of which 200,000 tons had been extracted by 1948. Along with coke ovens and other by-products. Mining finally came to an end at New Brancepeth colliery in 1953.

The first village school was built by the colliery owners in 1873, above the part of the village known as the "Low Side" a settlement comprising of the following streets:- Plantation Row, Hankey, Margaret, Hepworth and Regent streets and Colliery View occupied by the colliery's miners and their families, a primitive methodist chapel was established in 1884. To the south side of the colliery was a further development of colliery houses mainly occupied by the officials and craftsmen employed at the colliery. These colliery rows were called Sleetburn, Eshwood, Jubilee, Harvey and Church streets with Unthank Terrace and a private row of houses known as Fairfalls Terrace. A Wesleyan church was built at the end of Eshwood street in 1877, with St. Catherines church being built by 1890.

A miners institute was located in Unthank Terrace by 1890, and it later became the New Brancepeth working mens club, which claims to be the oldest club in County Durham. And just below the club was New Brancepeth Co-op store. In 1913, a new miners institute was built at Rock terrace which had an extensive library and other recreational facilities.

The central section of the village comprised of some private housing, the streets are called Edward Terrace, Co-operative Terrace, Benville Terrace and Bewley Terrace, which leads up to the New Brancepeth Hotel in later years known as the Tavern.

The Other two streets completing this central section being Rock Terrace and Walton Terrace, with Alum Waters located nearby. New Brancepeth has the distinction of having the first village nursery school in the country, opened in 1938.

New Brancepeth was located in the district of "Unthank" in more ancient times first appearing in records of 1314 and the low side was known as "Skutes House" (Scouts House) which was first mentioned in 1585 and owned by Ralph Richardson. The area is located now in the parish of Brandon and Byshottles, which forms part of the City of Durham District.

The villages former name of Sleetburn was dropped because it may have been confused with the name of Sleekburn in Northumberland, but is still affectionately known by its former name to this present day.

John R. Kitching

Portrait of Henry Heath Cochrane 1852 - 1924 (son of Brodie Cochrane and grandson of Alexander Brodie Cochrane the colliery founder) was the controlling force within the community, taking an active role in running the colliery and the village. Dissent was uncommon as all depended on him for their well being.

Mr Cochrane was known to send his manservant to any household that met his disapproval, if seen quarrelling, being drunk, or gossiping by housewives at their front doors! He dominated all aspects of village life, and kept control with the threat of withdrawing employment to any offending miner and his family, and the loss of their family home, which he provided for his workers.

Henry Heath Cochrane lived at Eshwood Hall for forty years, he died at a London nursing home in 1924. He was brought back to New Brancepeth for burial at Brandon Village Cemetery, alongside his first wife Millie. Although married twice he died without producing an heir to follow in his footsteps at New Brancepeth.

Wedding photograph of Henry Heath Cochrane in 1874

Eshwood Hall in 1908, residence of the Cochrane family, which was situated in nine acres of trees and parkland complete with artificial lake and ornamental garden pools.
The Hall was located at the end of 1 mile driveway and although situated in the vicinity of the colliery workings, it was screened by the landscape. The mineworks or the miners colliery rows could see nor be seen from Eshwood Hall. After the death of Henry Heath Cochrane, his wife resided at the Hall for a couple of years and it was demolished in 1927.

Eshwood Hall, 1905.
Meet of the North Durham Fox Hounds Mr. Cochrane can be seen wearing the tweed hat, he kept a fine stable of hunters and a full pack of hounds at Eshwood Hall.

Unthank Terrace, New Brancepeth. 3810

Unthank Terrace 1912, St. Catherines church can be seen to the left, and Eshwood Hall to the centre left. Eshwood Street is also on the left at the bottom of the bank, which stopped short of the driveway entrance to the Cochranes residence. On the right is Unthank Terrace, New Brancepeth Working mens Club was located midway down this terrace, which claims the distinction of being the oldest registered working mens club in County Durham. Below the club was New Brancepeth Co-op store. This roadway is known locally as the "Store Bank".

Leisure Hours "Snapshot"
Competition organised by the Daily Mail newspaper, C1950. The photograph was captioned "On Guard", it shows two young boys fishing in the River Deerness with an onlooker standing guard on the footbridge at the mill, near Alum waters.

New Brancepeth British School (known as the Colliery School).
All that remains today is the school house, which can be partly seen below the school. The school was opened in 1873 and closed in 1916. It was used for concerts and wedding parties until it was finally demolished in 1954.
The school had provision for 250 scholars and in 1890 the Headmaster was Mr Samuel Pilling.

New Brancepeth Colliery School Group 5, C.1902.

St. Catherines Church built in 1890 on land given by Lord Boyne at a cost of £2,000. The church was consecrated by Bishop Westcott on 11th September 1890. The church was part of the Parish of Brandon, being a chapel of ease to St. John the Evangelist located at Meadowfield. It was burnt down in 1942, by two schoolboys who entered the church, lit some candles which set fire to the interior fabric, burning the church to the ground.

St. Catherines hockey team 1909, seen here with the Reverend A. Sellwood.

New Brancepeth School F.C. 1936
Included in the team are:- From **L to R back row** G. Gibb, T. Hutchinson, R. Smith, T. Pearson and J. Richardson
From **L to R middle row** J. Charlton, R. Jackson, F. Shevels (Capt.) W. Taylor and R. Ramm.
From **L to R front row** K. Hindmarch, C. Gray
This team were league champions of Deerness Valley Schools League 1935-36 without loss of a point, in addition to winning the Durham County Schools Hospital Cup, Deerness Nursing Cup and Ushaw Moor Aged Miners Cup.

Jubilee Street
One of a number of Colliery Rows contained in the village.
Shortly after this photograph was taken this street was demolished in the 1960's

Peace Procession 1919, at New Brancepeth.
The photograph is inscribed "View From Mr. Shevels House"

New Brancepeth Miners Institute, 1913.

The unveiling of the war memorial after the First World War
Situated in the grounds of the Miners Institute. Dedicated to the villages fallen in the Great War of 1914-18 and later was inscribed with the names of the fallen from the Second World War, 1939-45.

Over Sixties, Christmas Party inside the Miners Institute, C.1970's

New Brancepeth Colliery, Miners Lodge Banner at the Durham Miners Gala, 1950.

Two cloth capped miners from New Brancepeth Colliery, 1920. The miner on the right is called Kelly.

General view of New Brancepeth Colliery, 1947.
The first shaft being sunk by Alexander Brodie Cochrane's New Brancepeth Colliery Co. Ltd in 1856, mining finally ceased in 1953.

This group of miners, pose with their safety lamps!
New Brancepeth Colliery, a safety lamp pit! C.1920's.

Horse keepers at New Brancepeth Colliery, C.1920.
A family affair at New Brancepeth Colliery, with Father William Dodds and sons Percy and Charlie Dodds.

New Brancepeth Colliery, 1902.
Showing two Babcock & Wilcox boilers which were installed and fired from waste heat from the coke ovens.

a. **The Colliery Winding Engine,** C.1900 steam driven, at one end of a combined building with the Power House, New Brancepeth Colliery.

b. **The Power House,** C.1900 with what appears to be a steam driven electricity generator and pump at New Brancepeth Colliery.

New Brancepeth Colliery coke oven workers C.1910.

Workers from New Brancepeth Colliery Cokeworks, 1929.
This photograph was taken by the yard foreman, Mr. W. Wilson at one end of the works Power Station.

The interior workings of New Brancepeth Colliery, C.1940's.

New Brancepeth Miners Lodge Banner at Durham Miners Gala, C1950.
With the Miners Hall at Red Hills, proudly displayed on the Lodge Banner.

Barytes Mill, New Brancepeth Colliery C.1950.
Barytes or "Heavy Spar" was first discovered at New Brancepeth in 1900.
It was extracted from vertical seams over two periods 1904-1921 and 1938-1948.
This photograph shows the mill in a derelict state after approx. 200,000 tons of this mineral had been mined.

General view of New Brancepeth Colliery and Cokeworks after reclamation of the site during the 1960's.

New Brancepeth Colliery Institute Silver Band, C.1902
Under the direction of band master W.M. Calvert and the secretary was F.W. Smith who lived at 21, Jubilee Street.

a. The ariel flight descends overhead from **Pithouse Down into New Brancepeth Colliery passing over Eshwood, Sleetburn Streets,** C.1940.

b. A second view shows the ariel flight entering the **colliery workings**.

New Brancepeth Juvenile Revellers Jazz Band
About to turn left into the display field at the New Brancepeth Jazz Band Carnival 19th September 1971.

a. **New Brancepeth Junior School Team**, C.1910. The only known member of the team is goalkeeper, Tom Mitchell.

b. **New Brancepeth J.M & I. School football team, 1972-73.** Winners of the Deerness Valley League, The Madgin Trophy and Ushaw Moor Aged Miners Cup. Included in the team are :- From **L to R back row** Teacher Mr. Smith, J. Lumley, K. McGrail, W. Cummins, R. McLean, G. Hardman and Teacher Mr. Wheatley.
From **L to R** front row, R. Green, N. Hindmarch, N. Maughan, D. Miller (Capt.), P. Staff, K. Kenny, B. Lumley.

New Brancepeth School, Dancing Display Team, C.1916.
The group includes:- Rene Craig, Freda Brown, Ella Young, Nellie Grey, Tom Anderson and David Simpson.

a. **New Brancepeth Womens Institute**, 1960s.
Birthday celebrations for their oldest member, Mrs. Miller inside the miners institute.

b. **New Brancepeth Womens Institute, winners of the Singing Festival,** C.1960.
Proudly display their silverware! Mrs. Witty, first right, front row can be seen. The W.I's longest serving member.

New Brancepeth Tavern, C.1950's.
Formally known as New Brancepeth Hotel.
The Tavern was demolished in 1996, Samuel Bewley was the Publican in 1894.
This Public House was owned by Vaux Breweries.

Annie and Bob Wetherhill, 1959.
Landlords of New Brancepeth Tavern 1957-59.
This photograph was taken in the back yard, near the gents toilets.

a. New Brancepeth Infants School Pagent for the Retirement of Head Teacher, Miss Pearson on 9th July 1954.
b. Lady Gainford with presents from Queen Mary, Christmas 1938. For the infants at New Brancepeth School.

A. E. Rowland Haulage Contractor Coal & Coke Merchants, with their depot and garage located at the top of store bank. The vehicle is one of the first commercials owned by this family business, and complete with hydraulic tipper.

New Brancepeth Cricket Team, C.1920.

Trying on the Gas Masks! 29th September 1938.

Nativity Play, Christmas 1956.
Inside St. Catherines Mission Hall.

a. **The official opening of New Brancepeth Nursery School, by Lord Eustace Percy** in 1938.
   This was the first village nursery School in the Country.
b. **A group of young children and helpers beside the slide at New Brancepeth Nursery School,** 14th March 1947.

Group of Chapel people, C.1920's
Doris Hepplewhite is sitting on her mothers knee wearing the bonnet, **Middle Row, First Right**.
The only known persons within the group! Note the wide variety of ladies headwear of the period which can be seen within this group.

Mr. Herbert Wood, co-op store manager seen here second from the left, poses with the rest of his brothers for this family photograph. New Brancepeth Co-operative & Industrial Society was established in 1877. Herbert succeeded his father Isaac who was store manager for 45 years. "The society paid the highest dividend of any Co-op in The Deerness Valley which was 22%". Originally founded in a house in Eshwood Street with the new store in Unthank Terrace, erected in the 1890's.

On the 25th July 1911, **Colonel Samuel Franklin Cody** landed his Bi-Plane at Pit House at approx. 5.00am. he was involved in a air race from London to Newcastle when his plane developed engine trouble and the wings being constructed of wood and linen were in need of repair. Eva & Bessie Hornsby were local milners who assisted with the repairs.

A large crowd of local people had gathered, excited and intrigued at this rare occasion. Colonel Cody had lodged overnight at Eshwood Hall, by invitation from Henry Heath Cochrane until the repairs were completed. Although he did not win the race, he still received a special prize as he had been in the lead up to the landing at Pit House. Colonel Cody was killed two years later while flying his water plane, when it crashed at Laffans Plain, near Aldershot.

Mr. William Taylor
First local Councillor from the village to become the Mayor of the City of Durham, 1981-82.